Animals
and Us

A Very Special Relationship

John Train and Linda Kelly

DISTRIBUTED BY
ANTIQUE COLLECTOR'S CLUB

EASTHAMPTON, MA   WOODBRIDE, U.K.

Packaging and Photo Research: M.T. Train
Design: Natasha Tibbott, Our Designs, Inc.
Prepress and Printing: ZoneS, Milano
© 2011 M.T. Train/Scala Books
No part of this publication may be
reproduced without permission
ISBN 978-1-905377-52-7

Contents

Introduction	1
Dogs	2
Cats	18
The Horse	32
Farm Animals	42
Birds	56
Wildlife	74
Insects	94
Water Creatures	104

Adam Names the Animals, English, 12th century.

Introduction

Since the cave paintings of early man our relationship with animals has been a source of inspiration. His old hound Argos is the first to greet Odysseus on his return from Ithaca; ox, ass and camel gather round the crib in nativity paintings; symbolic birds and beasts embellish Persian legends.

Our responses to the creatures that share our world include love — often reciprocated — curiosity, amusement, wonder, fear.

Here then are some writings on the subject that have particularly taken our fancy.

Dogs

A Walk With Roger

Finishing at last, I would slip from the table and saunter towards the gate, where Roger sat gazing at me with a questioning air. Together we would peer through the wrought-iron gates into the olive-groves beyond. I would suggest to Roger that perhaps it wasn't worth going out today. He would wag his stump in hasty denial, and his nose would butt at my hand. No, I would say, I really didn't think we ought to go out. It looked as though it was going to rain, and I would peer up into the clear, burnished sky with a worried expression. Roger, ear cocked, would peer into the sky too, and then look at me imploringly. Anyway, I would go on, if it didn't look like rain now it was almost certain to rain later, and so it would be much safer just to

sit in the garden with a book. Roger, in desperation, would place a large black paw on the gate, and then look at me, lifting one side of his upper lip, displaying his white teeth in lop-sided, ingratiating grin, his stump working itself into a blur of excitement. This was his trump card, for he knew I could never resist his ridiculous grin. So I would stop teasing him, fetch my match-boxes and my butterfly net, the garden gate would creak open and clang shut, and Roger would be off through the olive-groves swiftly as a cloud-shadow, his deep bark welcoming the new day.

Gerald Durrell,
My Family & Other Animals

Odysseus Returns: Argos

As they talked a dog lying there lifted his head and pricked his ears. This was Argos whom Odysseus had bred but never worked, because he left for Ilium too soon: Yet the instant Odysseus approached, the beast knew him. He thumped his tail and drooped his ears forward, but lacked power to drag himself ever so little towards his master. However, Odysseus saw him out of the corner of his eye and brushed away a tear, which he covered by quickly saying to Eumaeus in an off-hand way: "Strange, that they let such a hound lie on the dung-hill! What a beauty to look at!..." Eumaeus answered: "That is the hound of a man who died far from home...Put him on the trail and no quarry ever escaped him, not even in the densest thickets, so keen he was of scent. Now he has fallen low, his master having perished abroad..." With this...Argos the dog went down into the blackness of death, that moment he saw Odysseus again after twenty years.

Homer, *Odyssey*,
trans. T. E. Lawrence

Four Feet

I have done mostly what most men do
And pushed it out of my mind;
But I can't forget if I wanted to,
Four feet trotting behind.
Day after day, the whole day through
Whatever my road inclined.
Four feet said "I'm coming with you"
And trotted along behind,
Now I must go by some other road —
Which I shall never find —
Somewhere that does not carry the sound
Of four feet trotting behind.

Rudyard Kipling

Decorum

Best of all I remember an evening when Christian Bérard — always known as Bébé — painter, designer and book illustrator, gloriously unkempt, with hair to his shoulders and a bushy brown beard full of cigarette ash (twenty years later it would hardly have been noticed, but the style was rare indeed in the 1940s), turned up with his pet pug under his arm. Soon after his arrival, he put it on the floor, where it instantly deposited a formidable turd. Bébé, horrified, unhesitatingly — and to the immense admiration it must be said, of all around him — picked it up and put it in his pocket. My mother always said that it was the best example of good manners she had ever seen.

John Julius Norwich, *Trying to Please*

Galupka

Madame Olga Georges-Picot liked to spend some time in winter at the Hotel La Pace in Montecatini. Her beloved dachshund, Galupka, acquired an unwelcome skill, that of fishing the occasional carp out of the fountain in the center of the courtyard.

This provoked some indignation on the part of the management, quite aside from the carp.

An elderly Englishman had for some years observed this recurring scene with bemusement. He was friendly with the principals, including Galupka. When he died, he left a small endowment to indemnify the hotel for Galupka's depredations.

J.T.

Telepathy

The dog's "receiving set" far surpasses our own analogous apparatus. Everybody who understands dogs knows with what almost uncanny certitude a faithful dog recognizes in its master whether the latter is leaving the room for some reason uninteresting to his pet, or whether the longed-for daily walk is pending. Many dogs achieve even more in this respect. My Alsatian Tito, the great-great-great-great-great-grandmother of the dog I now possess, knew, by "telepathy," exactly which people got on my nerves, and when. Nothing could prevent her from biting, gently but surely, all such people on their posteriors. It was particularly dangerous for authoritative old gentlemen to adopt towards me, in discussion, the well-known "you are, of course, too young" attitude. No sooner had the stranger thus expostulated, than his hand felt anxiously for the place in which Tito had punctiliously chastised him. I could never understand how it was that this reaction functioned just as reliably when the dog was lying under the table and was therefore precluded from seeing the faces and gestures of the people round it: how did she know who I was speaking to or arguing with?

Konrad Lorenz

Man and Dog

Who's this — alone with stone and sky?
It's only my old dog and I —
It's only him; it's only me;
Alone with stone and grass and tree.

What share we most — we two together?
Smells, and awareness of the weather.
What is it makes us more than dust?
My trust in him; in me his trust.

Here's anyhow one decent thing
That life to man and dog can bring;
One decent thing, remultiplied
Till earth's last dog and man have died.

Siegfried Sassoon

Stealing The King's Dog

We must call upon you again for a Black Dog between greyhound and spaniel, no white about him, only a streak on his brest, and his tayl a little bobbed. It is His Majesties own Dog, and doubtless was stoln, for the dog was not born in England, and would never forsake His master. Whosoever finds him may acquaint any at Whitehal for the Dog was better known at Court than those who stole him. Will they never leave robbing his Majesty! Must he not keep a Dog? This dog's place (though better than some imagine) is the only place which nobody offers to beg.

Advertisement placed by Charles II in *Mercurius Publicus*, June 28, 1660

Charles II Sails

I went and Mr. Mansell and one of the King's footmen with a dog that the King loved (which shit in the boat and made me laugh to think that a King and all that belong to him are but just as others are), in a boat by ourselves, and so got on shore when the King did.

Samuel Pepys, *Diary*
May 25, 1660

Epitaph

Near this spot

Are deposited the Remains of one

Who possessed Beauty without Vanity,

Strength without Insolence,

Courage without Ferocity,

And all the Virtues of Man without his Vices.

This Praise, which would be unmeaning Flattery

If inscribed over human ashes,

Is but a just tribute to the Memory of

BOATSWAIN, a DOG

Who was born at Newfoundland, May, 1803,

And died at Newstead, Nov 18th, 1808.

Lord Byron

Fun & Games

At Emil's request, Pantaleone made the poodle Tartaglia go through all his tricks — and Tartaglia jumped over a stick, "spoke" — that is to say barked – sneezed, shut the door with his nose, dragged along his master's well-worn slipper and at last, with an old cuirass on his head, enacted the part of Marshall Bernadotte being subjected to a severe reprimand from the Emperor Napoleon — for treason. Napoleon was naturally portrayed by Pantaleone, and very faithfully portrayed. With his arms crossed on his chest, and a three-cornered hat pushed down over his eyes, he spoke coarsely and very sharply in French — and, heavens, what

French! Tartaglia sat all huddled up before his sovereign, his tail between his legs, blinking from shame, and screwing up his eyes under the peak of the cuirass which sat askew on his head. From time to time, as Napoleon raised his voice, Bernadotte would stand on his hind legs. '*Fuori, traditore!*'* exclaimed Napoleon at last, having quite forgotten, in his excessive fury, that he should maintain his part of a Frenchman to the very end. Bernadotte dashed headlong under the divan, and immediately jumped out again, barking delightedly, as if to indicate that the performance was over. The spectators laughed a great deal, and Sanin more than anyone.

Ivan Turgenev, *Spring Torrents*
trans. by Leonard Shapiro

*Be gone, traitor!

Fetch!

Lord Ferrers had a black labrador of which he was extremely fond. Each morning on the portico he gave a peculiar order to the dog, which bounded away, over the fields and through a wood. It made for the main London-to-Leicester railway line which ran through the Staunton Harold estate a mile off. The guard on the train from London would at a certain spot throw a copy of the Times out of the window. The dog caught it and brought it back in its mouth to his master. This was a regular matutinal procedure.

James Lees Milne,
Through Wood and Dale

Presidential Counsel

If you want a friend in Washington,
get a dog.

Harry S. Truman

Cats

Ode on the Death of a Favorite Cat Drowned in a Tub of Goldfishes

'Twas on a lofty vase's side,
 Where China's gayest art had dyed
 The azure flowers that blow;
Demurest of the tabby kind,
 The pensive Selima, reclined,
 Gazed on the lake below.

Still had she gazed; but 'midst the tide
Two angel forms were seen to glide,
 The Genii of the stream;
Their scaly armour's Tyrian hue
Thro' richest purple to the view
 Betrayed a golden gleam.

The hapless nymph with wonder saw:
A whisker first and then a claw,
With many an ardent wish,
She stretched in vain to reach the prize.
What female heart can gold despise?
What cat's averse to fish?

Presumptuous maid! with looks intent
Again she stretched, again she bent,
Nor knew the gulf between.
(Malignant Fate sat by, and smiled)
The slippery verge her feet beguiled,
She tumbled headlong in.

From hence, ye beauties, undeceived,
Know, one false step is ne'er retrieved,
And be with caution bold.
Not all that tempts your wandering eyes
And heedless hearts is lawful prize,
Nor all, that glisters, gold.

      Thomas Gray

A Tale of the Fianna

Finn McCool, hunting with his companions, stops at a peasant's hut to seek food and drink. A bear enters the room and lies down on the table. Each of Finn's companions, and finally Finn himself, tries to wrestle the bear off the table, but without success.

Then a cat appears, and hops on the table. The bear leaves. The repast can proceed.

In this tale the bear is death, and the cat is love.

J.T.

Going too Far

"Apropos to Lady Holland, in addition to all her further insults on the town, she has set up a huge cat which is never permitted to be out of her sight, and to whose vagaries she demands unqualified submission from her visitors. Rogers, it seems, has already sustained considerable injury in a personal affair with this animal. Brougham only keeps him or her at arm's length by snuff, and Luttrell has sent in his formal resignation of all further visits till this odious new favourite is dismissed from the Cabinet."

Thomas Creevey: The Creevey Papers,
December 15, 1803

Jeoffry

For I will consider my Cat Jeoffry.

For he is the servant of the Living God duly and daily serving him.

For at the first glance of the glory of God in the East he worships in his way.

For this is done by wreathing his body seven times round with elegant quickness.

For then he leaps up to catch the musk, which is the blessing of God upon his prayer.

For having done duty and received blessing he begins to consider himself.

For this he performs in ten degrees.

For first he looks upon his forepaws to see if they are clean.

For secondly he kicks up behind to clear away there.

For thirdly he works it upon stretch with the forepaws extended.

For fourthly he sharpens his paws by wood.

For fifthly he washes himself.

For sixthly he rolls upon wash.

For seventhly he fleas himself, that he may not be interrupted upon the beat.

For eighthly he rubs himself against a post.

For ninthly he looks up for his instructions.

For tenthly he goes in quest of food.

For having consider'd God and himself he will consider his neighbour.

For if he meets another cat he will kiss her in kindness.

For when he takes his prey he plays with it to give it a chance.

For one mouse in seven escapes by his dallying.
For when his day's work is done his business more properly begins.
For he keeps the Lord's watch in the night against the adversary.
For he counteracts the powers of darkness by his electrical skin and glaring eyes.
For in his morning orisons he loves the sun and the sun loves him.
For he is of the tribe of Tiger.
For the Cherub Cat is a term of the Angel Tiger.
For he has the subtlety and hissing of a serpent, which in goodness he suppresses.
For he will not do destruction, if he is well-fed, neither will he spit without provocation,
For he purrs in thankfulness, when God tells him he's a good Cat.
For he is an instrument for the children to learn benevolence upon.
For every house is incomplete without him and a blessing is lacking in the spirit.

Christopher Smart,
Jubilate Agno

Mrs. Hawkins

"Could write a book," said the Brigadier.

"Why don't you?"

"Can't concentrate."

"For concentration," I said, "you need a cat. Do you happen to have a cat?"

"Cat? No. No cats. Two dogs. Quite enough."

So I passed him some very good advice, that if you want to concentrate deeply on some problem, and especially some piece of writing or paper-work, you should acquire a cat. Alone with the cat in the room where you work.

I explained, the cat will invariably get up on your desk and settle placidly under the desk-lamp. The light from a lamp, I explained, gives a cat great satisfaction. The cat will settle down and be serene, with a serenity that passes all understanding. And the tranquility of the cat will gradually come to affect you, sitting there at your desk, so that all the excitable qualities that impede your concentration compose themselves and give your mind back the self-command it has lost. You need not watch the cat all the time. Its presence alone is enough. The effect of a cat on your concentration is remarkable, very mysterious.

The Brigadier listened with deep interest as he ate, his glaring eyes turning back and forth between me and his plate. Then he said, "Good. Right. I'll go out and get a cat." (I must tell you here that three years later the Brigadier sent me a copy of his war memoirs, published by Mackintosh and Tooley. On the jacket cover was a picture of himself at his desk with a large alley-cat sitting inscrutably beside the lamp. He has inscribed it 'To Mrs. Hawkins, without whose friendly advice these memoirs would never have been written — and thanks for introducing me to Grumpy.' The book itself was exceedingly dull. But I had advised him only that a cat helps concentration, not that the cat writes the book for you.)

Muriel Spark, *A Far Cry From Kensington*

Hodge

When I observed he was a fine cat, Dr. Johnson said, "why yes, Sir, but I have had cats I liked better than this." And then as if perceiving Hodge to be out of countenance, added "but he is a very fine cat, a very fine cat indeed."

Boswell, *Life of Johnson*

Epitaphum Felis

By the weight of the wearying years, and by grievous illness
Compelled, I come at last to the Lethean lake-side:
"Have thou Elysian suns" said Propserine smiling,
"Elysian meadows."
Nay, but if I deserve it, O kindly Queen of the silence,
Grant me this boon, one night to return to the homestead,
Home to return by night, and into the master's ear,
Whisper, Across the waste of Stygian waters
Your Felis, most faithful cat, still holds you dear.

John Jortin, 18th century,
trans. from the Latin by Seamus O'Sullivan

The Monk and his Cat,
Pangur Ban

Pangur, white Pangur, Hoe happy we are
Alone together, scholar and cat
Each has his own work to do daily;
For you it is hunting, for me study.
Your shining eye watches the wall;
My feeble eye is fixed on a book.
You rejoice, when my mind fathoms a problem.
Pleased with his own art, neither hinders the other;
Thus we live ever without tedium and envy.

9th century Irish poem,
trans. W.H. Auden

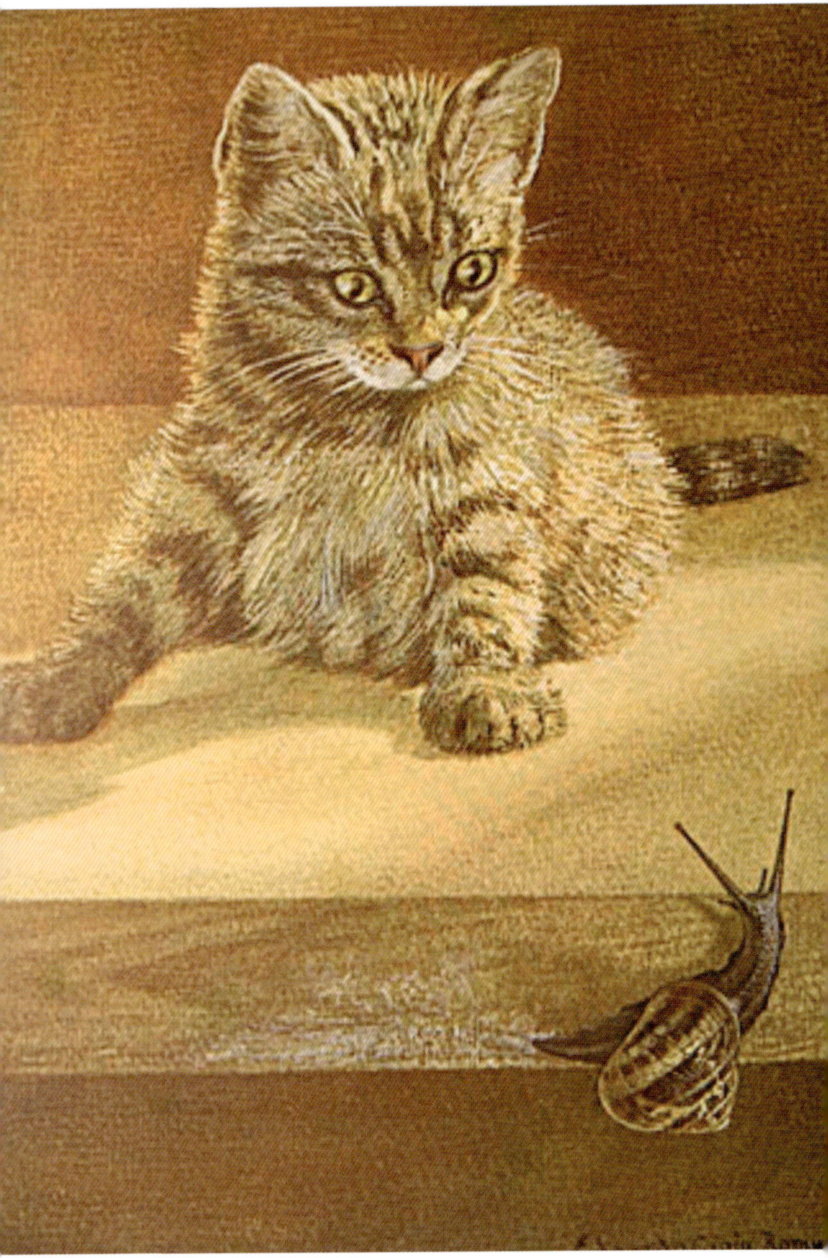

The Horse

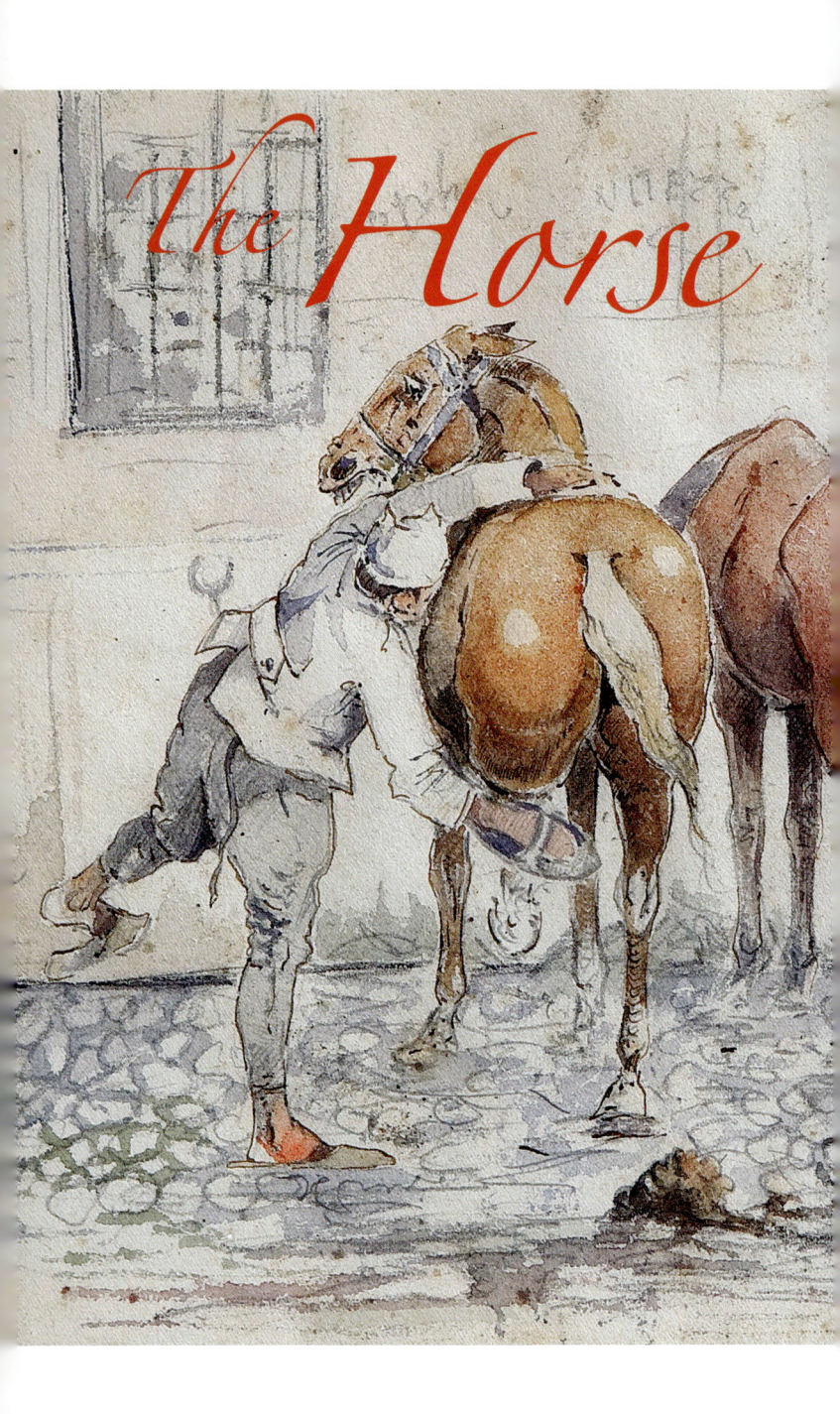

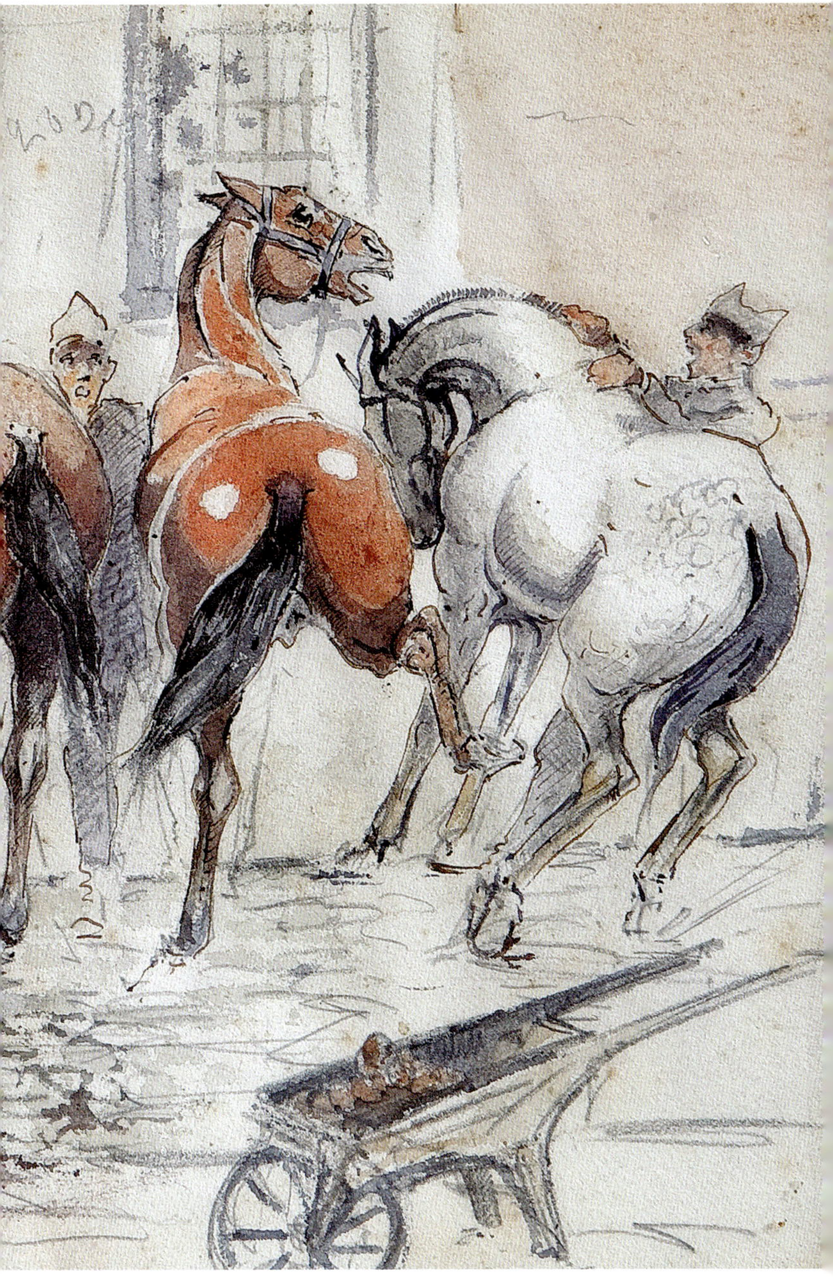

Lalla Feeling Frisky

"Why am I so nervous?" asked Stephen as he rode back towards Portsmouth. "My mind is in a silly flutter — pursues no clear line — flies off."

Since mood is so freely conveyed not only from person to person but from person to dog, cat, horse and the other way about, some part of his present state of mind derived from Lalla, though her unusual and nervous volatility arose from a cause that could not possibly have been more remote. The season of the year, her temperament, and a variety of other factors had inspired her with a notion that it would be delightful to meet with a fine upstanding stallion. She skipped as she went, sometimes dancing sideways, sometimes tossing her head: her views were evident to other members of her race, and poor rueful geldings rolled their eyes; while the only stone-horse they passed raced madly round and round his paddock, neighing; while a pretentious jack-ass uttered a huge sobbing cry that followed them beyond the cultivated land to the edge of a barren common where a broad lane joined their present road, the two running on to join the highway by a gallows. Pleased with her success, Lalla whinnied, arched her neck and curvetted to such a degree that Stephen cried "Avast, avast, there. Belay. Why, Lalla, for shame," and reined in hard to bring her to a halt.

Patrick O'Brian, *The Commodore*

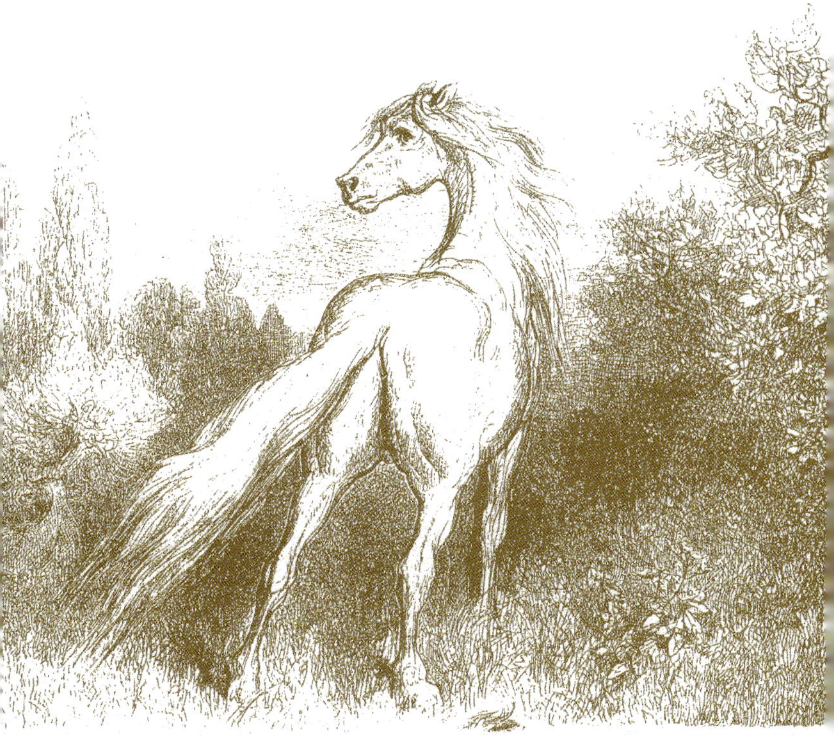

Warhorse

Hast thou given the horse strength? hast thou
clothed his neck with thunder?
Canst thou make him afraid as a grasshopper?
the glory of his nostrils is terrible,
He paweth in the valley,
and rejoiceth in his strength:
he goeth on to meet the armed men.
He mocketh at fear, and is not affrighted:
neither turneth he back from the sword.
The quiver rattleth against him, the glittering
spear and the shield.
He swalloweth the ground with fierceness and
rage: neither believeth he that it is the sound
of the trumpet.
He saith among the trumpets, Ha, ha: and he
smelleth the battle afar off, the thunder of
the captains and the shouting.

Book of Job

Maneuver

After the Battle of Waterloo, Sir Ashley Cooper, the famous London surgeon, attended the sale of the wounded horses, considered fit only for the knacker's yard. He bought 12 of the most serious cases, had them taken to his estate in Herefordshire, and began the systematic extraction of bullets and grapeshot. He saved the lives of all and turned them loose in his park. Then "one morning, to his great delight, he saw the noble animals form in line, charge, and then retreat, and afterwards gallop about, appearing greatly contented with the lot that had befallen them." These creatures had all served in different formations, and their self-taught skill was remarkable in itself. It was as though they grasped perfectly well that they had been through a horrific experience, so their exercises were a demonstration not only of their freedom of movement but their liberty of spirit: their masters had beaten the French, but they had overcome fate too.

Paul Johnson, in the *Spectator*

Before The Race

In the horse-box stood a dark bay mare, with a muzzle on, picking at the fresh straw with her hooves. Looking round him in the twilight of the horse-box, Vronsky automatically took in at one comprehensive glance all the points of his favourite mare. Frou-Frou was of a medium build, not altogether free from reproach, from a breeder's point of view. She was small-boned; her chest, although well arched, was narrow. Her hindquarters tapered slightly and in her fore-legs and still more in her hind-legs, there was a noticeable curvature. Neither her fore nor her hind legs were particularly muscular; but across the saddle she was exceptionally broad, owing to the training she had undergone and the leanness of her belly. Seen from the front her cannon-bones seemed no thicker than a finger but from the side they looked extraordinarily thick. Except for the ribs, she gave the impression of being all squeezed in at the sides and drawn out in depth. But she possessed in the highest degree that quality which made one forget the defects — that quality was blood, the blood that tells, as the English expression has it. The muscles showed sharply under the network of sinews covered with delicate, mobile skin, smooth as satin, and seemed as hard as bone. Her lean head with the prominent fiery eyes broadened out from the nose to the nostrils with their blood-red membranes. Her whole appearance, and in particular her head, was spirited yet gentle. She was one of those creatures who seem as if they would certainly speak if only the mechanism of her mouth allowed her to do so.

To Vronsky, at any rate, it seemed that she was understanding all he was feeling while he looked at her.

Leo Tolstoy, *Anna Karenina*,
trans. Rosemary Edmonds

Lower Mathematics

A horse that can count to ten is a remarkable horse, not a remarkable mathematician.

Samuel Johnson

Equine Information I

There is something in the outside of a horse that is good for the inside of a man.

Winston Churchill

Equine Information II

I know two things about the horse
And one of them is rather coarse

Naomi Royde-Smith, *Weekend Book*

Pride

Round-hoof'd, short-jointed, fetlocks shag and long,
Broad breast, full eye, small head, and nostril wide,
High crest, short ears, straight legs and passing strong,
Thin mane, thick tail, broad buttock, tender hide:
Look, what a horse should have he did not lack,
Save a proud rider on so proud a back.

William Shakespeare, *Venus and Adonis*

Farm Animals

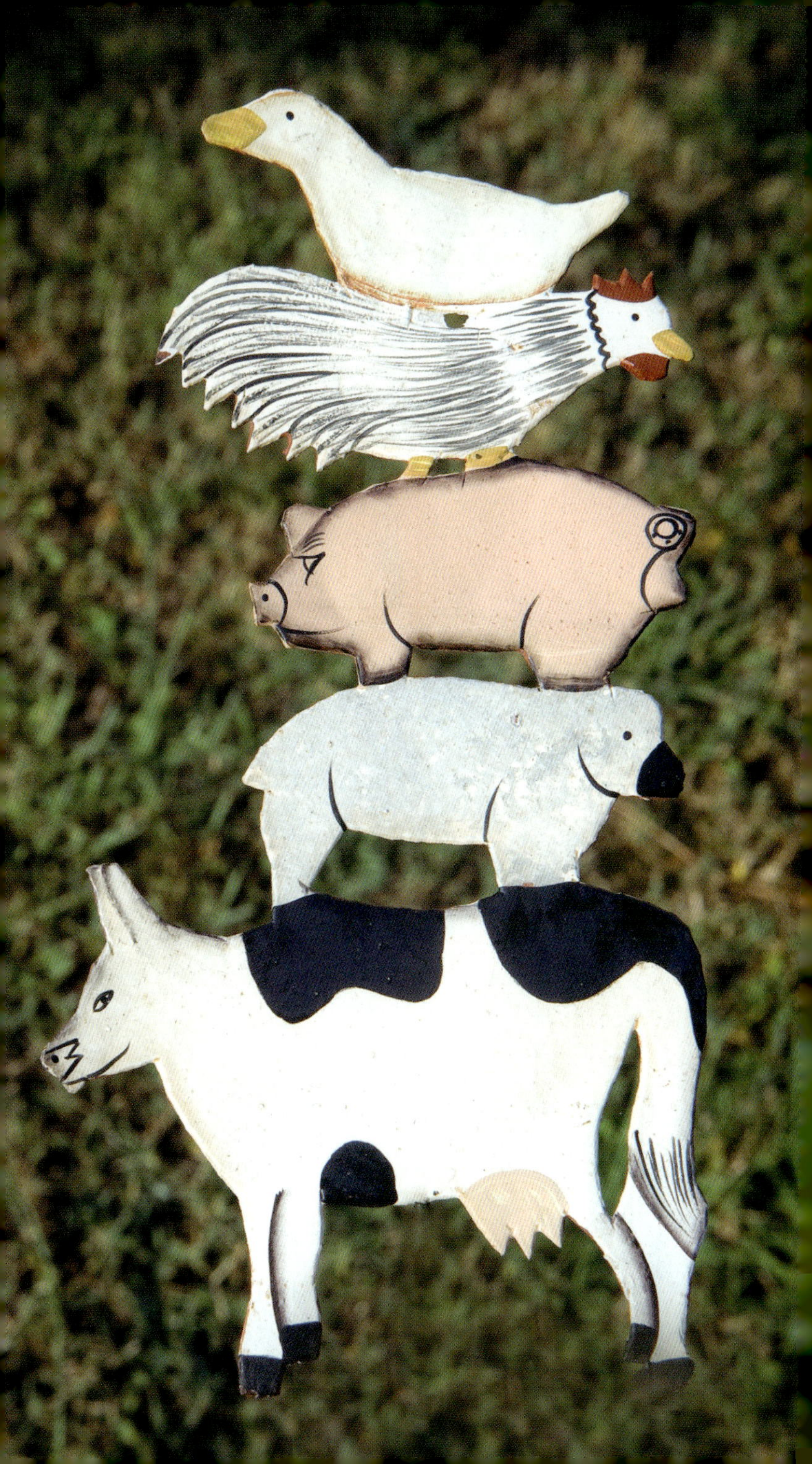

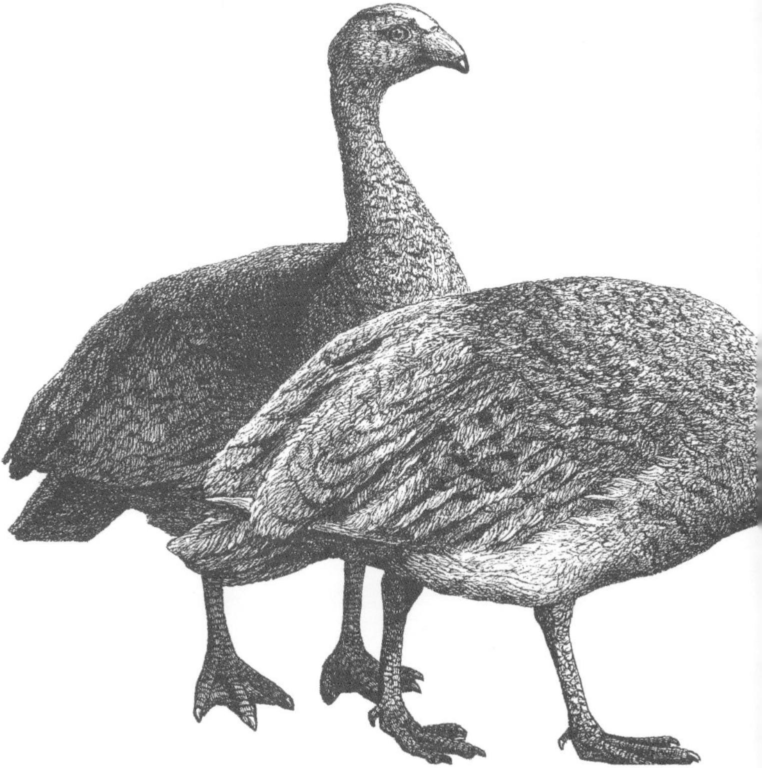

Conjugal Fidelity

Then there were the geese, the most admirable creatures I've ever met. We raised Chinese white geese, a common breed, and they have distinctive personalities. They mate for life and adhere to family values that would shame most of those who dine on them.

While one of our geese was sitting on her eggs, her gander would go out foraging for food — and if he found some delicacy, he would rush back to give it to his mate. Sometimes I would offer males a dish of corn to fatten them up — but it was impossible, for they would take it all home to their true loves.

Once a month or so, we would slaughter the geese. When I was 10 years old, my job was to lock the geese in the barn and then rush and grab one. Then I would take it out and hold it by its wings — on the chopping block while my Dad or someone else swung the ax.

The 150 geese knew that something dreadful was happening and would cower in a far corner of the barn, and run away in terror as I approached. Then I would grab one and carry it away as it screeched and struggled in my arms.

Very often, one goose would bravely step away from the panicked flock and walk tremulously toward me. It would be the mate of the one I had caught, male or female, and it would step right up to me, protesting pitifully. It would be frightened out of its wits, but still determined to stand with and comfort its lover.

Nicholas Kristoph

Trust

One of the most wonderful things I learnt [as a shepherd]… was the marvellous trust that exists between a shepherd and his sheep. It was a terrible day of blizzard and all the men were out on the fells trying to drive the sheep down to the safer places, and I was left in charge of the ones that were still in lamb. One sheep was trying to produce twins, and they were both jammed in her birth canal. I knew what I had to do but I was terribly afraid that I was hurting the sheep — and I probably was — but she knew me. I'll never forget the way she looked at me, over her shoulder, as if to say, "Go on, you're getting there!" And what was so lovely was that the next morning she came up with a beautiful lamb on each side of her as if to say, "Thank you very much."

Kate Rhodes, in a talk at the Wordsworth Trust

Sheep

The sheep ran huddling together against the hurdles, blowing out thin nostrils and stamping their delicate forefeet, their heads thrown back and a light steam rising from the frosty air.

Kenneth Grahame, *The Wind in the Willows*

The Donkey

When fishes flew and forests walked
And figs grew upon thorn,
Some moment when the moon was blood
Then surely I was born.

With monstrous head and sickening cry
And ears like errant wings,
The devil's walking parody
On all four-footed things.

The tattered outlaw of the earth,
Of ancient crooked will;
Starve, scourge, deride me: I am dumb,
I keep my secret still.

Fools! For I also had my hour;
One far fierce hour and sweet:
There was a shout about my ears,
And palms before my feet.

G.K. Chesterton,
The Donkey

Lord Gorbals

Once as old Lord Gorbals motored
Round his moors near John o' Groats
He collided with a goatherd
And a herd of forty goats.
By the time he had got through
They were all defunct but two.

Roughly he addressed the goatherd:
"Dash my whiskers and my corns!
Can't you teach your goats, you dotard,
That they ought to sound their horns?
Look, my AA badge is bent!
I've a mind to raise your rent!"

Harry Graham

The Hen

The Hen is a ferocious fowl,
She pecks you till she makes you howl.

And all the time she flaps her wings,
And says the most insulting things.

And when you try to take her eggs,
She bites large pieces from your legs.

The only safe way to get these,
Is to creep on your hands and knees.

In the meanwhile a friend must hide,
And jump out on the other side.

And then you snatch the eggs and run,
While she pursues the other one.

The difficulty is, to find
A trusty friend who will not mind.

Alfred Douglas

Adventitious Gesture

...Nothing much has happened to me except
I saw a rabbit yawn. I suppose people who
keep tame rabbits have seen it often but
this was a wild rabbit and I thought it a very
curious sight. It was a very bored triangular
yawn in the middle of a long hot afternoon.

C.S. Lewis

The Oxen

Christmas Eve, and twelve of the clock.
"Now they are all on their knees,"
An elder said as we sat in a flock.
By the embers in hearthside ease.

We pictured the meek mild creatures where
They dwelt in their strawy pen,
Nor did it occur to one of us there
To doubt they were kneeling then.

So fair a fancy few would weave
In those years! Yet, I feel,
If someone said on Christmas Eve,
"Come; see the oxen kneel,

"In the lonely barton by yonder coomb
Our childhood used to know,"
I should go with him in the gloom,
Hoping it might be so.

Thomas Hardy

The Cow

The friendly cow all red and white
I love with all my heart:
She gives me cream with all her might,
To eat with apple-tart.

She wanders lowing here and there,
And yet she cannot stray,
All in the pleasant open air,
The pleasant light of day;

And blown by all the winds that pass
And wet with all the showers,
She walks among the meadow grass
And eats the meadow flowers.

Robert Louis Stevenson

Rats

Split open the kegs of salted sprats,
Made nests inside men's Sunday hats,
And even spoiled the women's chats,
By drowning their speaking
With shrieking and squeaking
In fifty different sharps and flats.

Robert Browning,
from *The Pied Piper of Hamalin*

Hierarchy

I am fond of pigs. Dogs look up to us. Cats look down on us. Pigs treat us as equals.

Winston Churchill

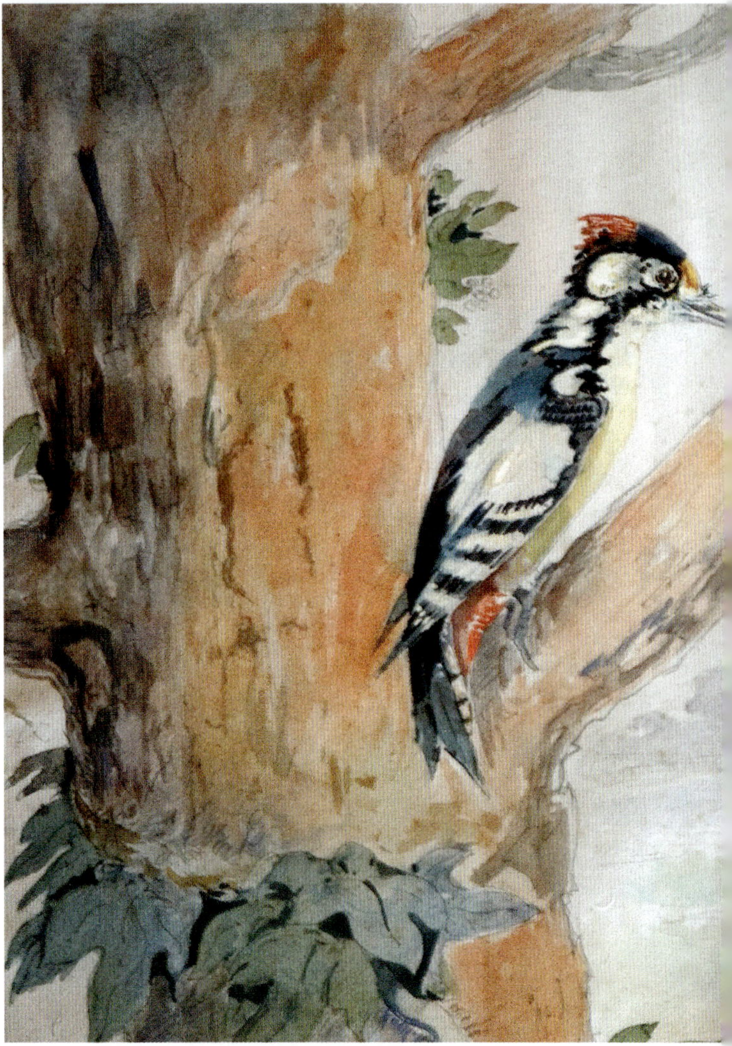

Birds

Cold

St. Agnes Eve — ah, bitter chill it was!
The owl, for all his feathers, was a-cold;
The hare limped trembling through the frozen grass,
And silent was the sheep in woolly fold...

John Keats,
The Eve of St. Agnes

The Owl's Cry

Downhill I came, hungry, and yet not starved;
Cold, yet had heat within me that was proof
Against the North wind; tired, yet so that rest
Had seemed the sweetest thing under a roof.

Then at the inn I had food, fire, and rest,
Knowing how hungry, cold, and tired was I.
All of the night was quite barred out except
An owl's cry, a most melancholy cry

Shaken out long and clear upon the hill,
No merry note, nor cause of merriment,
But one telling me plain what I escaped
And others could not, that night, as in I went.
And salted was my food, and my repose,
Salted and sobered, too, by the bird's voice
Speaking for all who lay under the stars,
Soldiers and poor, unable to rejoice.

Edward Thomas

The Eagle

He clasps the crag with crooked hands,
Close to the sun in lonely lands,
Ringed with the azure world he stands.
The wrinkled sea beneath him crawls,
He watches from his mountain walls,
Then like a thunderbolt, he falls.

                                  Alfred, Lord Tennyson

Wondrous Ways

There be three things which are too wonderful for me
Yea, four which I know not,
The way of an eagle in the air;
The way of a serpent upon a rock;
The way of a ship in the midst of the sea;
And the way of a man with a maid.

Ecclesiastes

Rapture

That's the wise thrush; he sings his song twice over
lest you should think he never could recapture
His first fine careless rapture...

Robert Browning,
Home Thoughts from Abroad

The Hoopoe

In Farid ud-Din's prodigious Conference of the Birds (*Mantiq at-Tair*), an immensely influential Sufi parable of the spiritual life, a flock of pilgrim birds engage the hoopoe to guide them to their king, the Simurgh.[1] As he describes the frightful hazards that lie before them, many of the candidates beg off: The self-centered parrot and peacock discover other concerns; the goose and bittern must stay by water; the nightingale's duty is to teach the mysteries of love and sing rapturously to the rose. The hoopoe has contempt for these excuses.

Eventually, led by the hoopoe, the birds cross the valleys of the quest for truth, of love, of mystical knowledge, of detachment and of unity, and the deserts of astonishment and annihilation. Many die or are lost.

Finally they reach the palace, only to find that they, si murgh, 30 birds, are the object of their own quest: Divine reality is within ourselves.

John Train,
Oriental Rug Symbols

---

[1] The mythical king of birds, a variation of the phoenix. The word derives from Avestan *saena marega*, "eagle bird." It is sometimes depicted as a combination of an eagle, dog and lion, merging with the griffin, an ancient and rich symbol signifying, among other things, the ascent of Alexander the Great to heaven.

Transference

Birds reared in isolation from their kind do not generally know which species they belong to; that is to say, not only their social reactions but also their sexual desires are directed towards those beings with whom they have spent certain impressionable phases of their early youth. Consequently, birds raised singly by hand tend to regard human beings, and human beings only, as potential partners in all reproductive activities.

This phenomenon can be observed regularly in hand-reared male house sparrows, who, for this reason, enjoyed great popularity amount the loose-living ladies of Roman society, and whom Catullus has immortalized by his little poem *"Passer mortuus est meae puellae."**

Konrad Lorenz

*The sparrow of my girl has died.

Full-Hearted

At once a voice arose amoung
The bleak twigs overhead
In a full-hearted evensong
Of joy illimited;
An aged thrush, frail, gaunt, and small,
In blast-beruffled plume, Had chosen thus to fling his soul
Upon the growing gloom.

So little cause for carolings
Of such ecstatic sound
Was written on terrestrial things
Afar or nigh around,
That I could think there trembled through
His happy good-night air
Some blessed Hope, whereof he knew
And I was unaware.

Thomas Hardy,
The Darkling Thrush

Swans

Among what rushes will they build,
By what lake's edge or pool
Delight men's eyes, when I awake some day
To find they have flown away?

* * *

The nineteenth Autumn has come upon me
Since I first made my count;
I saw, before I had well finished,
All suddenly mount
And scatter wheeling in great broken rings
Upon their clamorous wings.

W.B. Yeats,
The Wild Swans at Coole

Alternative Uses

The cormorant or common shag
Lays eggs inside a paper bag
The reason you will see no doubt
It is to keep the lightning out
But what these unobservant birds
Have never noticed is that herds
Of wandering bears may come with buns
And steal the bags to keep the crumbs.

       Christopher Isherwood

Crow Haiku

Autumn evening—
A crow on a bare branch

>Basho

Shore Birds Haiku

Guardian of the gate
Of Suma, how many nights
Have you awakened
At the crying of the shore birds
Of the Isle of Awaji?*

Minimoto No Kanemara,
trans. Kenneth Rexroth

---

* Kenneth Rexroth says, "This is my favorite Japanese poem. There is a parallel implied with the guardian of the gates of life, weary with the cries of souls migrating from life to life…"

Avian Autocrats

High ranking jackdaws interfere vigorously in the quarrel of two subordinates, as soon as the argument gets heated. The arbitrator is always more aggressive toward the higher ranking of the two original combatants. Thus a high-caste jackdaw, particularly the despot himself, acts regularly on chivalrous principles — where there's an unequal fight, always take the weaker side. Since the major quarrels are mostly concerned with nesting sites (in nearly all other cases, the weaker bird withdraws without a struggle), this propensity of the strong male jackdaws ensures an active protection of the nests of the lower members of the colony.

Konrad Lorenz

A Sparrow's Flight

"Such," he said, "O King seems to me the present life of men on earth, in comparison with that time which is to us uncertain, as if when on a winter's night you sit feasting with your ealdormen and thegns — a single sparrow should fly swiftly into the hall, and combing in at one door, instantly fly out through another. In that time in which it is indoors it is indeed not touched by the fury of the weather, but yet this smallest space if calmness being passed almost in a flash, from winter going into winter again, it is lost to our eyes. Somewhat like this appears the life of man; but of what follows or what went before, we are utterly ignorant."

The Venerable Bede

Nightingale I

How thick the bursts come crowding through the leaves!
Again — thou hearest?
Eternal passion!
Eternal pain!

Matthew Arnold

Nightingale II

Tiou, tiou, tiou, tiou — Spe, tiou, squa — Tio,
tio, tio, tio, tio, tio, tio, tix — Coutio, coutio,
coutio, coutio — Squo, squo, squo, squo — Tzu,
tzu, tzu, tzu, tzu, tzu, tzu, tzi — Corror, tiou,
squa, pipiqui — Zozozozozozo¬zozozozozozo,
zirrhading — Tsissisi, tsissisisisisisis — Dzoree,
dzoree, dzoree, tzatu, dzi — Dlo, dlo,
dlo, dlo, dlo, dlo, dlo, dlo, dlo — Quio,
trrrrrrrrr — Lu, lu, lu, lu, ly, ly, ly, ly, lie, lie,
lie, lie — Quio didl li lulylie — Hagurr, gurr,
quipio — Coui, coui, coui, couri, qui, qui,
qui, gai, gui, gui, gui — Goll, goll, goll, goll
guia hadadoi — Conigui, horr, ha diadia dill
si — Hezezezezezezezezezezezezezeze
couar ho dze hoi — Quia, quia, quia, quia,
quia, quia, quia, quia, ti Ki, ki, ki, io, io, io,
ioioioio ki — Lu ly li le lai la leu, lo, didl io,
quia — Kigaigaigaigaigaigaigai guiagaigaigai
couior dzio dzio pi.

Lescuyer, *Langage
et Chant des Oiseaux*

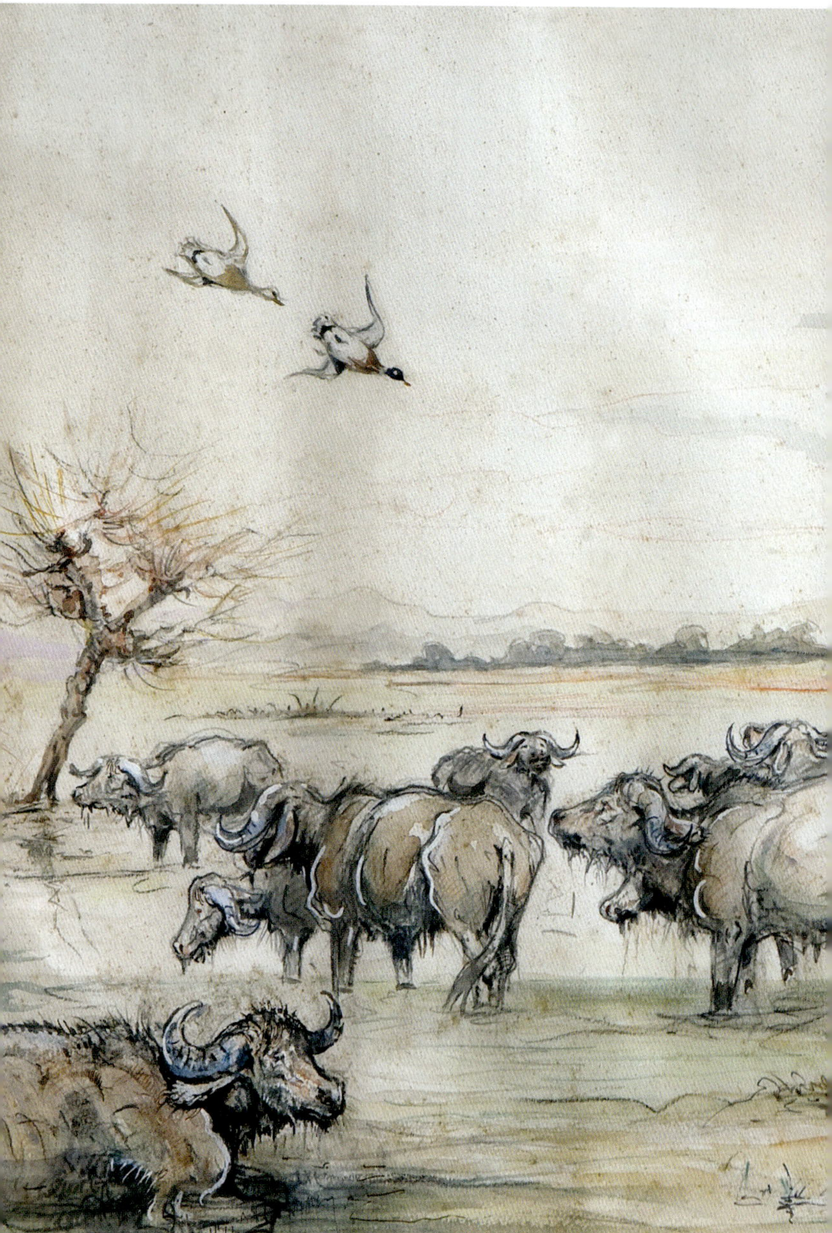

Wildlife

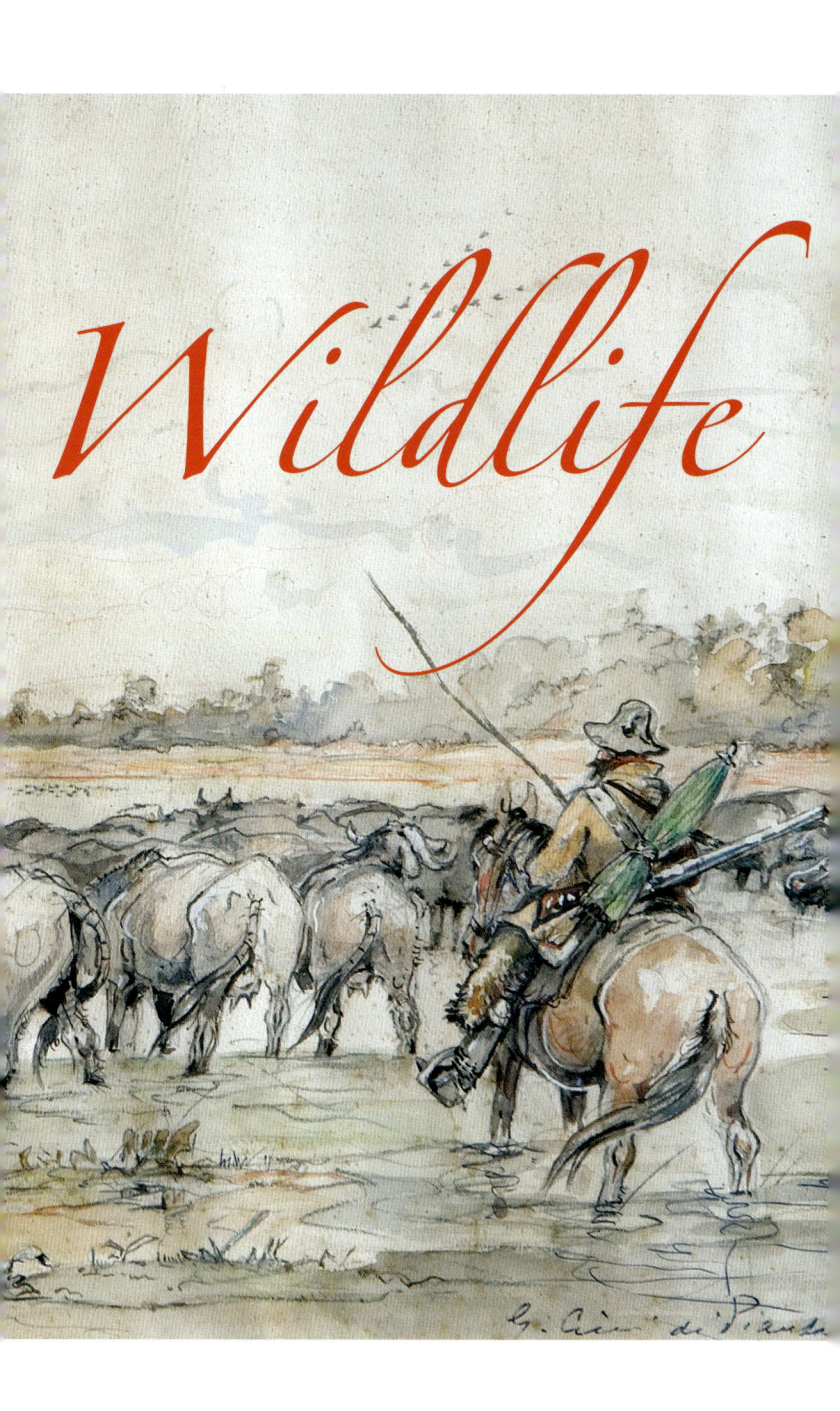

The Wolf and the Lamb

A lamb was quenching its thirst
In the water of a pure stream.
A fasting wolf came by, looking for something;
He was attracted by hunger to this place.
— What makes you so bold as to meddle with my drinking?
Said this animal, very angry.
You will be punished for your boldness.
— Sir, answered the lamb, let Your Majesty
Not put himself into a rage;
But rather, let him consider
That I am taking a drink of water
In the stream
More than twenty steps below him;
And that, consequently, in no way,
Am I troubling his supply.
— You do trouble it, answered the cruel beast.
And I know you said bad things of me last year.
— How could I do that when I wasn't born,
Answered the lamb; I am still at my mother's breast.
— If it wasn't you, then it was your brother.
— I haven't a brother. — It was then someone close to you;

For you have no sympathy for me,
You, your shepherds and your dogs.
I have been told of this. I have to make things even.
Saying this, into the woods
The wolf carries the lamb, and then eats him
Without any other why or wherefore.

                                          Jean de La Fontaine,
                                            trans. Eli Siegel

Scenting A Vixen

The fox's nose tipped up and round,
Since smell is a part of sight and sound.
Delicate smells were drifting by,
The sharp nose flaired them heedfully;
Partridges in the clover stubble,
Crouched in a ring for the stoat to stubble.
Rabbit bucks beginning to box;
A scratching pace for the pheasant cock
A hare in the read grass near the drain,
And another smell like the spring again.

A faint rank taint like April coming,
It cocked his ears and his blood went drumming,
For somewhere out by Ghost Heath Stubs
Was a roving vixen wanting cubs.
Over the valley, floating faint
On a warmth of windflaw, came the taint;
He cocked his ears, he upped his brush,
And he went upwind like an April thrush…

John Masefield, *Reynard the Fox*

The Tiger

Tiger, tiger, burning bright
  In the forests of the night,
    What immortal hand or eye
    Could frame thy fearful
    symmetry?

  In what distant deeps or skies
  Burnt the fire of thine eyes?
  On what wings dare he aspire?
What the hand dare seize the fire?

And what shoulder and what art
Could twist the sinews of thy heart?
And, when thy heart began to beat,
What dread hand and what dread feet?

What the hammer? what the chain?
In what furnace was thy brain?
What the anvil? What dread grasp
Dare its deadly terrors clasp?

When the stars threw down their spears,
And water'd heaven with their tears,
Did He smile His work to see?
Did He who made the lamb make thee?

Tiger, tiger, burning bright
In the forests of the night,
What immortal hand or eye
Dare frame thy fearful symmetry?

                        William Blake

Albert's Trip to the Zoo

…There was one great big lion called Wallace
His nose were all covered with scars
He lay in a somnolent posture
With the side of his face on the bars.

Now Albert had heard about lions
How they was ferocious and wild
To see Wallace lying so peaceful
Well, it didn't seem right to the child.

So straight way the brave little feller
Not showing a morsel of fear
Took his stick with the 'orse's 'ead 'andle
And shoved it in Wallace's ear.

You could see that the lion didn't like it
For giving a kind of a roll
He pulled Albert inside the cage with 'im
And swallowed the little lad 'ole.

Marriott Edgar,
Albert and the Lion

The Secret

It is apparently extremely difficult to breed lions in captivity, but there was at one time in the Dublin zoo a keeper by the name of Mr. Flood who had bred many lion cubs without losing one. Asked the secret of his success, Mr. Flood replied, "Understanding lions." Asked in what consists the understanding of lions, he replied, "Every lion is different."

John Wisdom

The Otter Surfaces

"What are you looking at?" said the Rat...

"I am looking," said the Mole, "at a streak of bubbles that I see travelling along the surface of the water. That is a thing that strikes me as funny."

"Bubbles? Oho!" said the Rat, and chirruped cheerily in an inviting way.

A broad glistening muzzle showed itself above the edge of the bank and the Otter hauled himself out and shook the water from his coat.

Kenneth Grahame,
The Wind in the Willows

To a Mouse
On Turning her up her Nest with the Plough

Wee, sleekit, cow'rin', tim'rous beastie,
O what a panic's in thy breastie!
Thou need na start awa sae hasty,
Wi' bickering brattle!
I wad be laith to rin an' chase thee
Wi' murd'ring pattle!

Thou saw the fields laid bare an' waste
An' weary winter comin' fast,
An' cozie here, beneath the blast,
Thou thought to dwell,
Till, crash! the cruel coulter past
Out thro' thy cell.

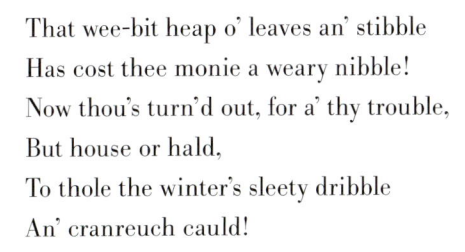

That wee-bit heap o' leaves an' stibble
Has cost thee monie a weary nibble!
Now thou's turn'd out, for a' thy trouble,
But house or hald,
To thole the winter's sleety dribble
An' cranreuch cauld!

But, Mousie, thou art no thy lane
In proving foresight may be vain
The best laid schemes o' mice an' men
Gang aft a-gley,
An' lea'e us nought but grief an' pain,
For promis'd joy.

Robert Burns

Friendly Hedgehog

Talking of animals a hedgehog came into our kitchen the other night. It didn't seem to be in the least afraid and drank a saucer of milk: when it had finished it got into the saucer and settled down to sleep just as if it intended to pass the night there!

> C.S. Lewis writing to his godson,
> Laurence Harwood

Just Gliding

Got my luncheon at Fresh Pond, and went back again to the woods. After much wanderings and seeing of many things, four snakes gliding up and down a wallow for no purpose that I could see — not to eat, not for love, but only gliding.

Ralph Waldo Emerson

Comparison

The Llama is a woolly sort of
fleecy hairy goat,
With an indolent expression and
an undulating throat
Like an unsuccessful literary man.

Hilaire Belloc

The Ibex

A member of the goat family, it has extraordinary jumping powers. A young specimen can leap from a standing start onto a man's head and stay there.

J.T.

Friendly Consultation

A French fable has it that the King convoked the animals of his domains and addressed them genially.

"I have assembled you, dear friends, to help deliberate on a matter of perennial importance to the Court, namely, how is it best that you should be cooked?

After a considerable silence, a small voice was heard from the back: "But we don't want to be cooked!"

The King glared at the speaker and thundered, "You wander from the point!"

J.T.

Poser

If animals weren't meant to be eaten,
then why are they made out of meat?

Jody Brown

Simian Anthropomorphism

It seems that animals always behave in a manner showing the rightness of the philosophy entertained by the man who observes them...Throughout the reign of Queen Victoria all apes were virtuous monogamists, but during the dissolute twenties their morals underwent a disastrous deterioration.

Bertrand Russell

The Elephant's Revenge

The most notable elephant in Greek history, called Victor, had long served in Pyrrhus's army, but on seeing its mahout dead before the city walls [at the battle of Tarentum, 280 BC], it rushed to retrieve him; hoisting him defiantly on its tusks, it took wild and indiscriminate revenge for the man it loved, trampling more of its supporters than its enemies.

Robin Lane Fox, *Alexander the Great*

Sagacious Pachyderm

The Romans held that the elephant was affectionate, honorable and reverent, and understood human speech.

One particular elephant would trace in the sand, "I, the elephant, wrote this."

J.T.

Chinese Saying

Kill the chicken to
frighten the monkey
(that is, make a
threatening gesture
of deterrence.)

J.T.

Slow Motion

The sloth, in its wild state, spends its life in trees, and
never leaves them but from force or accident. The eagle to
the sky, the mole to the ground, the sloth to the tree; but
what is most extraordinary he lives not upon the branches,
but under them. He moves suspended, rests suspended,
and passes his life in suspense — like a young clergyman
distantly related to a bishop.

Rev Sydney Smith, reviewing
Wanderings in America by Charles Waterton.

Subjective Evaluation

Cet animal est très méchant. Quand
on l'ataque, il se défend.*

Anon.

*This is a very wicked animal. If you attack
him, he fights back.

R.I.P.

My raven's dead. He had been ailing for a few days but not seriously, as we thought, and was apparently recovering, when symptoms of relapse occasioned me to send for an eminent medical gentleman one Herring (a bird fancier in the New Road) who promptly attended and administered a powerful dose of castor oil. This was on Tuesday last. On Wednesday morning he had another dose of castor oil and a tea cup full of warm gruel, which he took with great relish and so far recovered his spirits as to be enabled to bite the groom severely. At 12 o'clock at noon he took several turns up and down the table with a grave, sedate air, and suddenly reeled. This made him thoughtful. He stopped directly, shook his head, moved on again, stopped once more, cried in a tone of remonstrance and considerable surprise, "Holloa old girl!" and died.

He has left a rather large property (in cheese and halfpence) buried, for security's sake, in various parts of the garden. I am not without suspicions of poison. A butcher was heard to threaten him some weeks since and he stole a clasp knife belonging to a vindictive carpenter which was never found. For these reasons, directed at post mortem examination, preparatory to the body being stuffed; the result of it has not yet reached me.

Charles Dickens to Captain Basil Hall,
March 6, 1841

Disempathy

The philosopher Thomas Nagel wrote an essay titled "What Is It Like to Be a Bat?" in which he pointed out the difficulty of imagining what it would be like for him to be a bat (how it would feel to hang upside down in the dark, or to fly about and steer by sound, and so on) and the utter impossibility of imagining what it is like for a bat to be a bat.

Larissa MacFarquhar

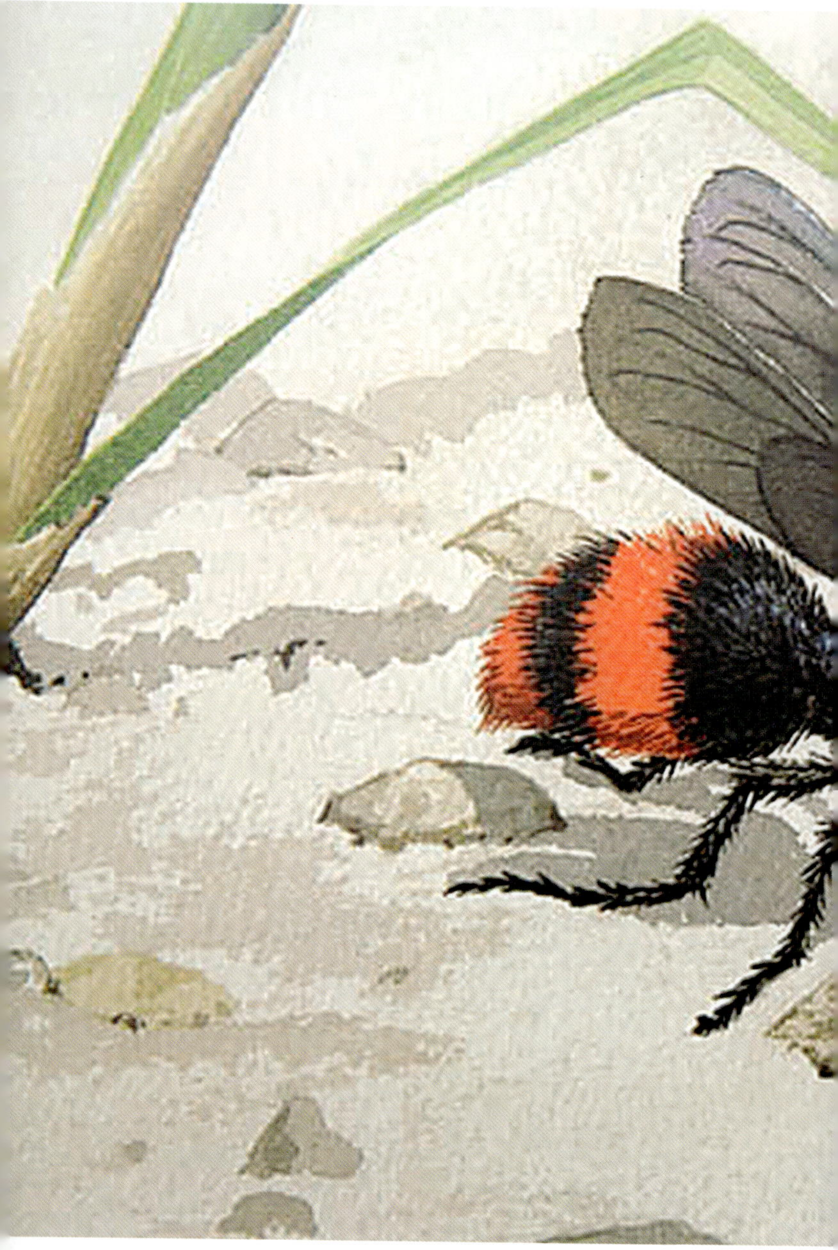

Insects

Beetlemania

An English theologian once asked the noted evolutionist J.B.S. Haldane what could be inferred about the mind of his Creator from the works of nature. Haldane replied, "An inordinate fondness for beetles."

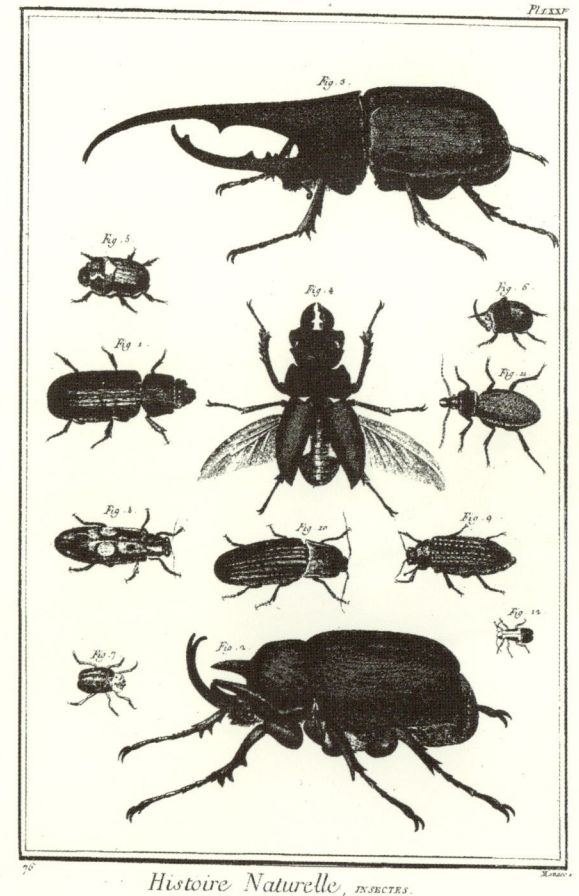

Histoire Naturelle, INSECTES.

Summer's Play

Little fly,
Thy summer's play
My thoughtless hand
Has brushed away.

Am not I
A fly like thee?
Or art not thou
A man like me

For I dance
And drink and sing,
Till some blind hand
Shall brush my wing.

If thought is life
And strength and breath
And the want
Of thought is death

Then am I
A happy fly,
Or if I live
Or if I die.

William Blake,
Songs of Experience

Here Be Swarms

Herodotus maintained that the countries north of the Black Sea — including present-day Ukraine — were so densely beset by swarms of furious bees that one could not penetrate there.

J.T.

Frustrated Zeal

One day, on tearing off some old bark I saw two rare beetles and seized one in each hand; then I saw a third and new kind, which I could not bear to lose, so I put the one which I held in my right hand into my mouth. But alas! It ejected some intensely acrid fluid that burnt my tongue so I was forced to spit it out and so it was lost.

Charles Darwin, *Autobiography*

The Cricket and the Ant

The cricket having sung
all summer long
found her groceries all too few
when again the north wind blew.
Nowhere could she spy
a scrap of worm or even fly.
So to her neighbor ant she fled
For a little help to plead:
Just a crumb to stay alive,
Until the warm days should revive.

"By August next I promise you
Principal and interest, too."

Now, the ant no lender is:
Of her faults that is the least.
"What were you up to in the summer?"
"Night and day, to every corner
I sang, whenever I'd a chance."

"So you sang, did you?
How sweet! Now dance."

Jean de La Fontaine,
Fables, trans. J.T.

The Blind Archimedes

On the burning ground of Africa, an individual termite fries; but assembling the requisite number of them triggers (through "quorum sensing") a prodigious building impulse. Chemical signals direct an orgy of wonderfully organized construction. These tiny cathedral-builders pile up columns and throw across connecting arches, erecting mounds hard as masonry and higher than a man.

Underground chambers and passageways delve hundreds of feet into the dark below the parched surface to find water and create a cool, moist indestructible habitat that shelters the colony for decades — all blind, but collectively the master mason.

J.T.

Little Pets

I dined today at Lord Erskine's... He told us that he had two favourite leeches. He had been blooded by them when he was dangerously ill in Portsmouth last autumn; they had saved his life and he had brought them with him to town — he had ever since kept them in a glass — and he himself everyday gave them fresh water and had formed a friendship with them. He said he was sure they both knew him and were grateful to him. He had given them different names, Home and Cline (the names of two celebrated surgeons).

Sir Samuel Romilly, quoted in Campbell's
Lives of the Lord Chancellors

Last and Least

He prayeth best who loveth best
All things both great and small;
The streptococcus is the test
I love him least of all.

Hilaire Belloc

Bees

When Mrs. Gorm — Aunt Eloise — was
stung to death by savage bees

Her husband, Prebendary Gorm, put on
his veil and took the swarm.

He's publishing a book next May called,
"How to Make Beekeeping Pay."

                        Harry Graham

Water

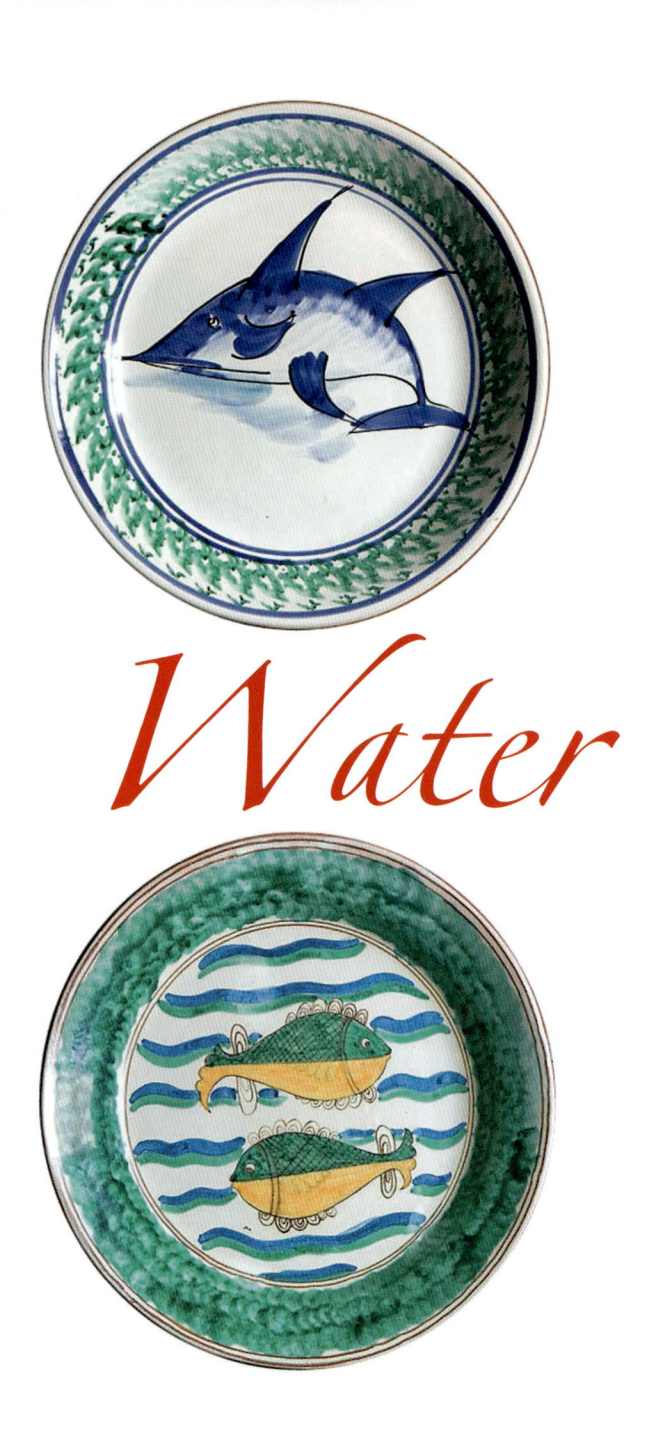

Creatures

Pet

The romantic poet Gerard de Nerval walked a lobster on a blue ribbon through the gardens of the Palais Royal. When asked why he chose such a strange creature as a pet he replied, "Because he does not bark and he knows the secrets of the deep."

L.K.

The Crocodile

How doth the little crocodile
Improve his shining tail,
And pour the waters of the Nile
On every golden scale!

How cheerfully he seems to grin!
How neatly spread his claws,
And welcomes little fishes in
With gently smiling jaws!

Lewis Carroll,
Alice in Wonderland

Whale's Greeting

When overflowing with mutual esteem, the whales salute each other *more hominem.*[*]

Herman Melville

[*]Like people.

Dolphins

The Greeks held that dolphins were men, transformed into that shape by Bacchus.

J.T.

Troubled Sea

That dolphin-torn,
That gong-tormented sea…

W.B. Yeats, *Sailing to Byzantium*

Kin

A new look at the brain of the porpoise was provided by Ridgeway, N.J. zoologists Sam H. Flanigan and James G. McCormick who claimed that the truly critical feature is not the gross weight but the relationship between weight of brain and weight of spinal cord. Roughly speaking, the brain is the seat of reasoned behavior; the cord of reflexive. Some of the huge dinosaurs had a brain the size of a walnut, but a massive cord. The team has dissected fifteen porpoises of three species. Their figures on comparative brain-to-cord ratios were: fishes, less than 1; horse, 2.5; cat, 4 or 5; apes, 8; porpoises, 36; man, 50. These finding show the porpoise as closest to the human.

Victor B. Scheffer

Fish Heaven

Fish (fly-replete, in depth of June,
Dawdling away their wat'ry noon)
Ponder deep wisdom, dark or clear,
Each secret fishy hope or fear.
Fish say, they have their Stream and Pond;
But is there anything Beyond?
This life cannot be All, they swear,
For how unpleasant, if it were!
One may not doubt that, somehow, Good
Shall come of Water and of Mud;
And, sure, the reverent eye must see
A Purpose in Liquidity.
We darkly know, by Faith we cry,
The future is not Wholly Dry.
Mud unto mud! — Death eddies near —
Not here the appointed End, not here!
But somewhere, beyond Space and Time.
Is wetter water, slimier slime!
And there (they trust) there swimmeth One
Who swam ere rivers were begun,
Immense, of fishy form and mind,
Squamous, omnipotent, and kind;
And under that Almighty Fin,
The littlest fish may enter in.
Oh! never fly conceals a hook,
Fish say, in the Eternal Brook,
But more than mundane weeds are there,
And mud, celestially fair;
Fat caterpillars drift around,
And Paradisal grubs are found;
Unfading moths, immortal flies,
And the worm that never dies.
And in that Heaven of all their wish,
There shall be no more land, say fish.

Rupert Brooke

Bad Idea

It would be like urging a jellyfish to grit its teeth and dig in its heels. The poor creature lacks the rudimentary organs for such as an operation.

Hugh Trevor-Roper

Salmon Leap

O to break loose, like the chinook
Salmon jumping and falling back,
Nosing up to the impossible
Stone and bone-crushing watherfall —
Raw-jawed, weak-fleshed there, stopped by ten
Steps of the roaring ladder, and then
To clear the top on the last try,
Alive enough to spawn and die.

Robert Lowell,
Waking Early Sunday Morning

Frog Haiku

An old pond —
A frog
Kerplop!

      Basho

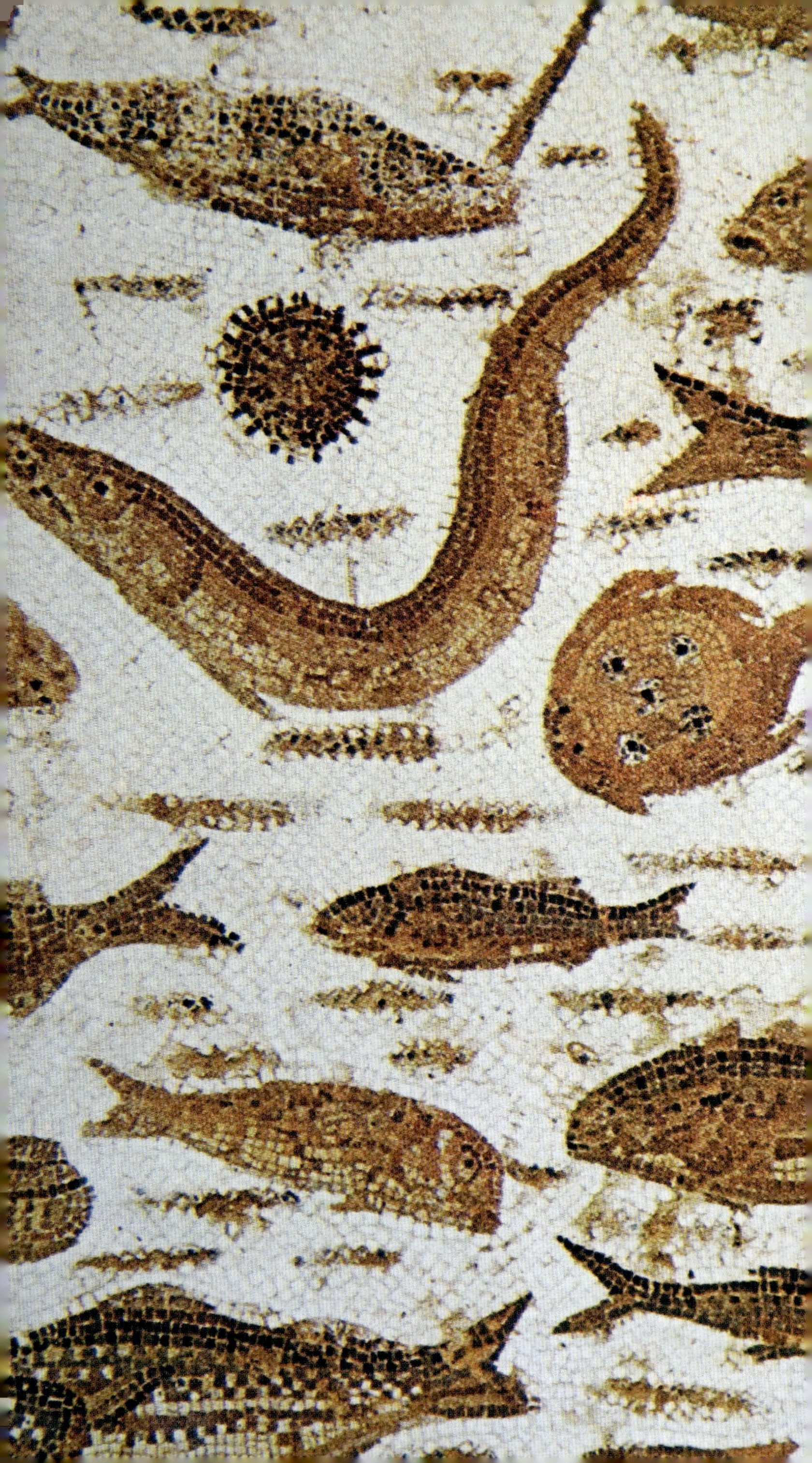

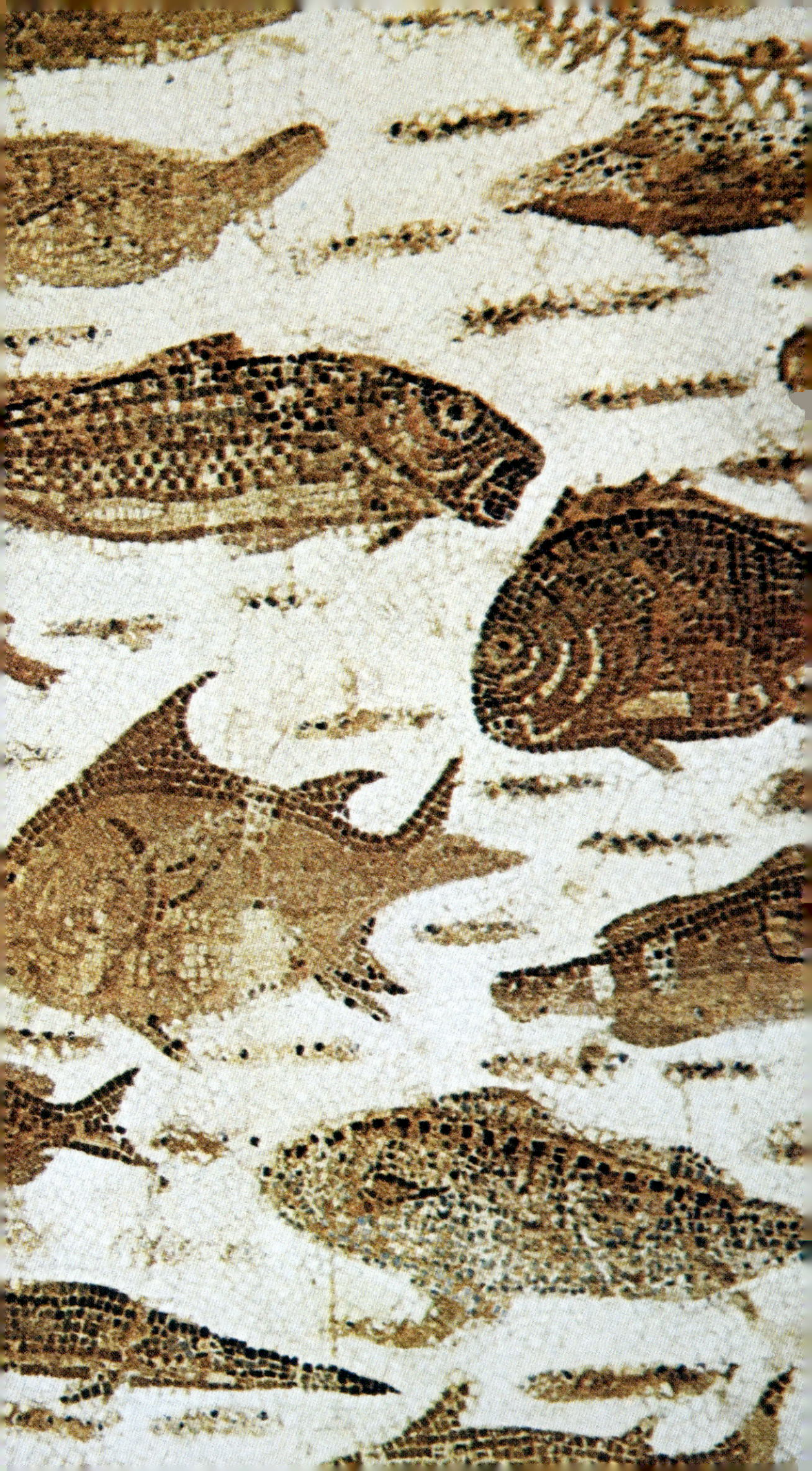

John Train has written hundreds of columns in the *Wall Street Journal*, *Forbes*, London's *Financial Times*, and other publications, as well as over 20 books on many subjects. Also a number of amusing "little books," including *John Train's Most Remarkable Names*, *Most Remarkable Occurrences*, *Wit: The Best Things Ever Said*, *Love*, and others, which have proven to be perennially-popular stocking stuffers.

He has received several appointments from Presidents of both parties. He and his wife live in New York and Maine.

Linda Kelly's previous books include *The Young Romantics*, *Women of the French Revolution* and *Richard Brinsley Sheridan*. She is a Fellow of the Royal Society of Literature and of the Wordsworth Trust. Her husband is the writer Laurence Kelly; they live in London and spend some time in Ireland, where they have a cottage on the Wexford coast.